YOU CHOOSE
BOOKS™

AT BATTLE IN THE CIVIL WAR

AN INTERACTIVE BATTLEFIELD ADVENTURE

by Allison Lassieur

Consultant:
James McPherson
Professor of American History, Emeritus
Princeton University, Princeton, New Jersey

CAPSTONE PRESS
a capstone imprint

You Choose Books are published by Capstone Press,
1710 Roe Crest Drive, North Mankato, Minnesota 56003
www.capstonepub.com

Library of Congress Cataloging-in-Publication Data
Lassieur, Allison.
  At battle in the Civil War : an interactive battlefield adventure / by Allison Lassieur.
      pages cm. — (You choose books. You choose: battlefields.)
  Summary: "In You Choose format, explores the Civil War from the view of infantry,
artillery, and cavalry soldiers"—Provided by publisher.
  Includes bibliographical references and index.
  ISBN 978-1-4914-2149-9 (library binding)
  ISBN 978-1-4914-2391-2 (paperback)
  ISBN 978-1-4914-2395-0 (eBook PDF)
1. United States—History—Civil War, 1861–1865—Juvenile literature. 2. Soldiers—
United States—History—19th century—Juvenile literature. 3. Soldiers—Confederate
States of America—Juvenile literature. I. Title.
  E468.L27 2015
  973.7—dc23   2014023840

Editorial Credits
Mari Bolte, editor; Tracy Davies McCabe and Charmaine Whitman, designers;
Wanda Winch, media researcher; Laura Manthe, production specialist

Photo Credits
(Clubs are Trumps) by Dale Gallon, Courtesy of Gallon Historical Art,
www.gallon.com, cover, (The Hornets' Nest) by Dale Gallon, Courtesy of Gallon
Historical Art, www.gallon.com, 45; Bear River Homestead: James Martin, 23;
Bridgeman Images/Private Collection/Robert Marshall Root, 6; Corbis: Bettmann,
15, ©Medford Historical Society Collection, 8, 91; CriaImages.com: Jay Robert Nash
Collection, 30–31, 42, 73, 84, 102; Getty Images: Hulton Archive/Three Lions,
21, MPI, 88; James P. Rowan, 52, 66; Library of Congress: Prints and Photographs
Division, 27, 48, 55, 61, 64, 100; National Archives and Records Administration, 12,
70; North Wind Picture Archives, 10, 36; www.historicalimagebank.com, Painting by
Don Troiani, 78, 98

Printed in Canada.
092014   008478FRS15

TABLE OF CONTENTS

4

ABOUT YOUR
ADVENTURE

The Civil War (1861–1865) was a major conflict in American history. It was fought with the most modern weapons and tactics the world had ever seen. The weapons killed men by the thousands. When the war ended, nothing was the same.

In this book you'll explore how the choices people made helped to win, or lose, the Civil War. The events you'll experience happened to real people.

Chapter One sets the scene. Then you choose which path to read. Follow the directions at the bottom of each page. The choices you make will change your outcome. After you finish one path, go back and read the others for new perspectives and more adventures.

YOU CHOOSE the path
you take through history.

Abraham Lincoln felt it was his presidential duty to preserve the Union at all costs—even if that meant going to war.

1

THE FIRST MODERN WAR

For four years the Civil War tore the country apart. When it was over, everything had changed.

It was a war over states' rights and slavery. In the South, slavery flourished. Wealthy planters owned hundreds of slaves. In the North, slavery was illegal. Many people were against slavery and wanted it abolished everywhere.

In 1860 Abraham Lincoln was elected president. He said he would not end slavery in states where it already existed. But the southern slave states didn't believe him. One by one they left the Union and formed the Confederate States of America. This divide led to the Civil War.

Turn the page.

Neither side was ready for war. They scrambled to raise armies. Factories rushed to make the most modern weapons and artillery.

The North had five times more factories than the South. In 1860 only 3 percent of the firearms in the United States were made in the South.

Over the war years, a single Union foundry produced more than 2,000 cannons and 3 million shells.

But the South had strengths too. They had a great number of trained officers. At the time there were eight military colleges, and only one was in the North. They were also fighting in their own territory, giving them home field advantage.

Both armies had infantry, artillery, and cavalry brigades. The infantry were the foot soldiers. Most Civil War soldiers on both sides were infantrymen. The artillery soldiers fired and maintained the big guns. Cavalrymen rode into battle on horseback and served as guards, spies, and scouts.

9

To be an infantryman at the Battle of Shiloh, turn to page 11.

To fight as an artillery soldier at the Battle of Chattanooga, turn to page 49.

To ride into battle as a cavalry soldier at the Battle of Gettysburg, turn to page 79.

When the war began, the North and South had armies of almost equal size.

2
SOLDIERS OF WAR

You'll never forget November 6, 1860. On that day, Abraham Lincoln was elected president. In the North, people celebrated. In the South, people rebelled. They hated President Lincoln for one reason: his belief against slavery. Many southerners owned slaves. They were afraid that Lincoln would make slavery illegal.

Soon after, southern states began to secede. The first to leave the Union was South Carolina. In just a few weeks, six other southern states—Mississippi, Florida, Alabama, Georgia, Louisiana, and Texas—had seceded. They called themselves the Confederate States of America.

Turn the page.

On April 12, 1861, Confederate forces bombed the Union-held Fort Sumter in South Carolina. The battle raged for 34 hours before the Confederates won. After the battle, Virginia, Arkansas, North Carolina, and Tennessee joined the Confederacy. Both sides realized they had a real war on their hands.

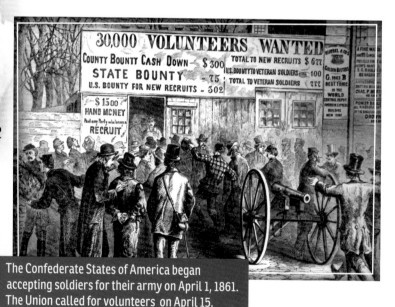

The Confederate States of America began accepting soldiers for their army on April 1, 1861. The Union called for volunteers on April 15.

One day a poster appears in the town's general store. "Volunteers!" it screams in huge black letters. "To arms! Your country calls! All those who desire to join with us in serving our country, now is the time!" The poster says that all recruits should report to the store the next day.

No one on either side thinks the war will last very long. So you'd better sign up quick, before you miss out. Everyone you know is joining up and leaving home. Your mother weeps and begs you not to go, but you can't stay home. The thought of battle, with guns blazing and cannons exploding, is thrilling!

13

To join as a Confederate infantry recruit, turn to page 14.

To sign up as an infantry solider in the Union army, turn to page 32.

People are already signing up when you arrive at the store. You know almost everyone. Old men, young boys, and farmers are ready to fight. You wonder if there will be any men left in town by the end of the day. Two officers sit behind a table. One of them is the town's mayor.

"We're forming an infantry company of 100 men," the mayor says. "I'll be your captain."

"We'll join up with nine other Alabama companies to make one infantry unit," the other officer says. "The pay is $11 a month. Make your mark here." There are several "X" marks on the paper from people who don't know how to read or write. You know how, so you proudly scrawl your name. Suddenly someone claps you on the shoulder. It's your friend Clem.

"We're soldiers now!" he says happily. "Let's go shoot some Yankees!"

The officer behind the table laughs. "You can't do that without a gun," he says. "Later, there might be enough money for army weapons. For now, though, you have to bring your own."

You have no rifle. The idea of going home and facing Mother again is not good.

Men between the ages of 18 and 45 were the ideal age to enlist.

To go home to get a rifle, turn to page 16.

To borrow a rifle from Clem, turn to page 18.

Your mother's tear-stained face greets you at the door. She disappears into her bedroom and comes out with a bundle wrapped in a blanket. Inside is a rifle.

"This was your daddy's gun when he fought in the Mexican-American War," she says. "It's an 1841 rifle musket. It's old, but it still works." There's also a Bowie knife and a small pistol. She puts them all in your pack, along with ammunition. She clutches the pack to her chest for a moment before giving it to you.

You can't look back as you step off the porch. All the excitement of going to war drains away with your mother's tears. Is this what happened when your father went to war? What went through his mind as he turned his back on his family? Was his choice this hard?

16

To reconsider, go to page 17.

To head to war, turn to page 19.

The dusty road into town seems to lead to glory and excitement. Staying means facing people who will call you a coward. But maybe there are worse things than being called a coward. You turn around.

Your mother's look of shock and surprise makes you smile. "I can't leave you like Daddy did," you say. Slowly you remove the weapons. "I'm going to stay here and take care of you and the farm."

Your mother collapses, sobbing with relief. In the distance you hear the sound of drums as the soldiers in town gather in camp. You may get in trouble later for backing out, but you've made the right choice for your family.

THE END

To follow another path, turn to page 9.

To read the conclusion, turn to page 103.

Clem sees you hesitate. "Don't worry," he says. He hands you an old rifle. "You can use this. It's an 1841 from the Mexican-American War. Lots of soldiers are using these old weapons. They may have seen better days, but they'll still kill plenty of Yankees!"

"Thanks, friend," you say as he tosses you a box of ammunition. You catch it in midair and push it into your pack.

"Don't mention it," Clem says. "Just be sure to shoot first. I don't want to drag your sorry carcass off some field somewhere."

You both laugh, but your stomach lurches with fear. For an instant your head fills with an image of bodies lying bloody and broken on a battlefield. Quickly you shake it off. That's not going to happen to you.

The glory of war beckons too strongly. Soon it's time to get on the train. The whole town cheers and claps as a band plays a lively tune. Girls throw flowers and swoon as you pass.

"You're so brave," one girl sighs. She presses a small sewing kit called a "housewife" into your hand. It contains a needle and thread and small bits of fabric. You tuck it into your pocket.

You see your mother in the crowd, waving with an embroidered hanky. She looks both proud and sad.

Soon the town is far behind. A few days later, the train passes a long line of white tents. It's the main camp of your new regiment. The other infantry companies are already here. It's time to learn how to be a soldier.

19

To start marching drills, turn to page 20.

To practice shooting, turn to page 22.

May 1861

Dearest Family, I am writing just a few lines to let you know that I am safe. The regiment has been camping here for several weeks. All we do is drill, drill, drill. They want us to be organized when battle comes, but it is slow and boring work. Some men turn to gambling and drink to pass the time. Of course, I don't partake in that!

Drums wake us at 5 a.m. After roll call and breakfast, we march side-by-side. Drummers keep the beat, which helps. We learn commands to stand at attention, to face right and left, and to fire our weapons. Some soldiers don't have guns yet. They carry broomsticks instead.

After marching, those of us who do have guns practice loading and firing. Once one practice is over, another begins. We drill most of the day. Yesterday it rained all day but we drilled anyway.

Letters were the only way a soldier could communicate with his family. However, they were also usually the only way a soldier's family would learn of his death.

Many men have measles. There is so much sickness in camp that the officers built a wooden two-story hospital. I am fine. I will write again when I am able.

You don't have the heart to tell your mother that you're feeling sick too. After all, by the time she gets your letter, you may be feeling well again. But the next morning you've got a fever, runny nose, cough, and a rash.

21

To go to the hospital, turn to page 24.

To stay in the tent, turn to page 25.

Once everyone is in line, the quartermaster hands out brand new rifles.

"This here beauty is a Pattern 1853 Enfield Rifle-musket," the captain says. "They came all the way from England, where they are made. So take good care of them, boys."

The gun weighs only nine pounds, and it's accurate. The best thing is that the rifle can shoot minié balls, a new bullet that will do a lot of damage to the enemy. Each cone-shaped bullet has four grooves in the bottom. Its shape allows it to fly faster and straighter. It does more damage on impact than an ordinary bullet too. But after a few rounds the quartermaster stops everyone.

"No need wasting minié balls on practice," he says. "Save them for battle. I'm sure you'll shoot straight when you're shooting at Yankees!" Everyone laughs and cheers in agreement.

After a lesson in how to clean and store your gun, drill is over. Soon after, word spreads through the ranks. The regiment marches out tomorrow. Battle is coming.

Millions of bullets were fired during the Civil War. At least 7 million bullets were used during the Battle of Gettysburg alone.

Turn to page 26.

The doctor shakes his head when he examines you. "Measles," he says. "At least a quarter of the men have it." He puts you into a bed on the second floor of the hospital. It's the first real bed you've seen in weeks. With a sigh you fall asleep.

A huge crash wakes you in the night. Rain pounds and lightning flashes. Suddenly the whole building shudders. You feel like you're floating before everything goes dark.

When you come to, you are in a different bed in a different building. Bandages cover your head, arms, and legs. A tired orderly notices that you're awake. "The hospital collapsed in the storm," he says. "You were badly hurt, but you will survive. You're going home, son." The war is over for you before it even begins.

24

THE END

To follow another path, turn to page 9.

To read the conclusion, turn to page 103.

You lay miserable in your tent all day. Clem brings you water and some food, but it hurts to swallow and you're not hungry. At one point the doctor appears. You think you hear the word "measles," but you're too sick to care.

It takes more than a week for you to feel better. Finally you can swallow some bread and hot coffee. Clem tells you that many men have fallen sick and died. "It's all us country boys," Clem says. "We ain't never had these diseases like they do in the big cities."

You're feeling much better by the next morning. It's a good thing, too, because the order to march comes down. Maybe that means you're going to battle at last.

Turn the page.

The army marches for days. The troops sing songs and crack jokes all day. At night in camp you all play cards and talk of how many Yankees you're going to kill. You've never had so much fun in your life!

Late one evening, the army is ordered to stop. You're now within a mile of the enemy line, at a place called Shiloh. Everyone is ordered to keep his weapon close. You awake before dawn. You're shaking, but you're not sure if it is because of excitement or fear.

Clem spies some violets on the ground. "Let's put them in our caps," he says. He's talking a little too loudly. He's nervous too. "Maybe the Yankees won't shoot us if we're wearing these. They are a sign of peace, after all." You stick a few purple flowers in your cap, but your hand is shaking so much that you drop some.

The air explodes with gunfire. It's all you can do not to throw yourself on the ground. But you swallow hard and keep moving. Bullets hum and zing past you, hitting the trees. Twigs and leaves rain down over your head, stinging your eyes and scratching your skin. Smoke fills the air. Soon can't see more than a few feet in front of you.

The Battle of Shiloh is also known as the Battle of Pittsburg Landing. It lasted two days.

Turn the page.

"Aim low," the officer says. "You're more likely to hit something that way." You shoot into the smoke as you advance. Explosions shake the ground and the air is filled with pops of gunfire. Then the smoke clears. One by one, soldiers in blue coats are exposed.

Your line rushes forward, every man yelling at the top of his lungs. You turn to Clem. He has a strange look on his face. Blood pours from his side as he crumples to the ground.

28

To stay with Clem, go to page 29.

To stay with the line and fight, turn to page 30.

Clem is dead in minutes. You cradle his head in your lap and gently wipe the blood from his face. He doesn't look dead. Part of you waits for him to open his eyes and laugh at the joke he's played on you. But you know that's impossible. Tears blur your vision.

You've never seen death up close like this. If this is war, you don't want any part of it. A bullet tears your cap right off your head. The next one hits you in the shoulder. The pain is unbearable—the minié ball shattered the bone on impact. But soon the pain is gone and you feel nothing. You fall to the ground and bleed to death next to your friend, violets scattered around you.

29

THE END

To follow another path, turn to page 9.

To read the conclusion, turn to page 103.

There's nothing you can do for Clem. He'd want you to avenge him. There is so much gunfire that the captain orders everyone to take cover. You load and fire until your hands are sore. Your eyes sting and begin to water.

It's hard to breathe with all the smoke and gunpowder, but you try not to cough. Breathing at the wrong time could mess up your aim, and you want to make your shots count.

Union soldiers swarmed the Confederate defense lines.

A line of blue coats appears through the smoke. You look for your fellow Confederates, but they're all dead or they retreated. You are alone and surrounded by Yankees.

"Don't shoot!" you shout, dropping the gun. Two soldiers grab you by the collar, take your gun, and march you to their camp. You're a prisoner of war. But you're alive, for now.

THE END

To follow another path, turn to page 9.

To read the conclusion, turn to page 103.

The whole town is in a frenzy. You go to the town square to see what's happening. Crowds of people are there, waving flags and cheering. The town band plays a lively tune. A man in a bright blue uniform stands on a table and shouts, "Sign up here for the Great War Adventure!"

Before you know it, you have signed the papers. One by one, dozens of men enlist. You all clap and cheer one another. Pretty girls give you flowers and kiss your hand. They sigh and bat their eyes when you dashingly promise that you'll fight for them. You already feel like a hero.

It's a different story at home. When you break the news that you've enlisted, your mother's face goes pale. She doesn't look proud or happy at all as she begs you to change your mind.

"You're my only child," she says. "I don't know what I would do if you were killed. Nothing is worth that, not even keeping the Union together."

Your father is a pacifist. He would rather discuss issues than fight over them. You know he doesn't want you going to war.

To ask your father's opinion, turn to page 34.

To enlist despite your parents wishes, turn to page 36.

"I admire your courage," he begins. "But this war isn't going to last long. The rebels will come running back to the Union the first time they see blood. And your mama is broken up. I'm asking you not to go, for her. If this war does go on, there will be a need for soldiers later."

Your mother hugs you when you nod. "But I'm not going to wait forever," you vow.

Every day the wait gets harder. The papers bring more news about the war. You are furious when you hear of the stunning Union defeat at the Battle of Manassas in July. You could have been there. You could have been the difference.

Just as you make up your mind to enlist, you are accepted into Harvard University. Education is important. But the Union needs you.

To go to school, go to page 35.

To go to war, turn to page 36.

It was a hard decision but in the end Father convinced you that education should be your first priority. "The war will be over one day," he said before you left home. "But a good education will last a lifetime."

Many Harvard students and graduates have already left for war. Secretly, you're a little relieved to be here instead of on the battlefield. Some of your friends have died. You could have been one of them. Maybe if the war is still going on when you graduate, you'll enlist.

THE END

To follow another path, turn to page 9.

To read the conclusion, turn to page 103.

The next day you report back to town. You have to get checked over to make sure you're fit for duty. The doctor makes you jump, bend over, and kick. He checks your eyesight and your teeth.

"Congratulations," he says. "Welcome to the army." He hands you a piece of paper that says you're healthy. You'll start training the next day.

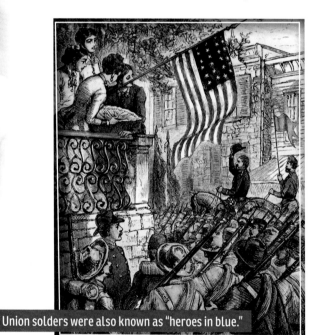

Union solders were also known as "heroes in blue."

To learn how to shoot, go to page 37.

To learn how to march and fight in battle, turn to page 40.

You're up before dawn. Officers hand out new muskets.

"What you hold in your hands, boys, is the Springfield .58 caliber," the officer brags. "It can kill at 1,000 feet. It shoots minié balls, the best ammunition for killing rebels."

The officer starts shouting commands. Each command is a step in loading and firing your new gun.

"LOAD!" The officer shouts. You hold your rifle muzzle-up, with the butt on the ground.

"HANDLE CARTRIDGE!" You take a paper packet filled with gunpowder from your cartridge pouch.

"TEAR CARTRIDGE!" You tear the cartridge packet with your teeth. You are careful not to spill the gunpowder.

Turn the page.

"CHARGE CARTRIDGE!" You pour the gunpowder into the rifle's muzzle. Then you add a minié ball. The empty paper packet goes on top of the minié ball.

"DRAW RAMMER!" You grab the rammer, a long thin metal rod. When the officer shouts, "RAM CARTRIDGE!" you use the rammer to pack the gunpowder tight in the rifle's muzzle.

"RETURN RAMMER!" You return the rammer to its position.

"PRIME!" With your thumb, you cock the hammer of the rifle halfway. You put a percussion cap onto the cone. The percussion cap will cause a spark that will light the gunpowder.

"READY!" You use your thumb to cock the gun's hammer all the way back.

"AIM!" You put the rifle butt against your shoulder and aim for the target.

"FIRE!" With a squeeze of the trigger, you make your shot.

Now everyone must wait for the last command—"RECOVER ARMS!" That means it's time to reload and fire again.

You'll be expected to shoot 2 to 3 times a minute. You're beginning to reach that goal when the officer ends practice for the day.

You spend weeks in camp practicing drill after drill. More recruits sign up. In the spring the order comes to move out.

39

Turn to page 42.

The commander, Colonel Hugh Thompson Reid, watches as the soldiers start drill. First everyone jostles one another into two long lines, shoulder to shoulder. The back row is only about an arm's length from the front row.

"They aren't going to shoot us in the back, are they?" one soldier in the front row asks.

"No, soldier. They shoot over the shoulders of you men in the front row," Colonel Reid explains. "This way both lines can fire at once. Just think, if all of you shoot three rounds a minute, that's 40,000 ounces of lead going straight into the enemy lines!"

The lines erupt into hoots and hollers. You wave your cap and shout, "Let's show those rebels who's in charge!" Colonel Reid smiles and calms everyone down.

An officer says that sometimes one or two companies will be ordered to break out of line and move forward. "You'll either look for surprise attacks or fight smaller groups of rebels," he says.

You spend hours marching in line and learning commands. Finally drill is over. Colonel Reid calls everyone together.

"I've received orders. We're to move out tomorrow," he says.

Turn to page 42.

You march to St. Louis. Boats take you to join Ulysses S. Grant's army in Tennessee. Booms and shouts greet you when you land. You have arrived in the middle of a battle!

The regiment forms a long line on a bluff overlooking the river. Are you the only one who is confused and terrified? One look at the wide-eyed faces of the other soldiers gives you the answer.

More than 6,000 soldiers were killed during the Battle of Shiloh. In total there were about 23,000 casualties.

An officer hands out ammunition. Your heart races as you load your gun. Your shaking hands make loading even more difficult.

Riderless horses pour out of the woods, swerving around you. A moment later, wounded men follow. They are covered in blood and gore. The sight is horrific. Some of the soldiers in line throw up from the sight.

A badly injured soldier grabs your arm. "Don't go out there," he croaks before dying at your feet. Other wounded men moan for help.

43

To stay with the regiment, turn to page 44.

To help a wounded soldier, turn to page 47.

Someone gives an order, but you can't hear what it is. Everyone starts marching, so you do too. Bullets whistle past your ear. Some hit your fellow soldiers. You hit the ground as cannon fire blasts. The regimental flag flutters to the ground, shot full of holes. Nobody makes a move to replace the flag bearer, who is also full of holes. It seems to be every man for himself.

Fear overcomes you. Crawling on the ground, you and a few others take cover. All you can do is lie there, trembling. Someone shakes you. "Get up, fool," he growls. "Do you want to die on your belly or with a gun in your hand?"

He pulls you up and shoves your gun at you. You blindly load and fire until the bullets and cartridges are gone. You have no idea if you're hitting anything, but at least you're doing something. It's better than sitting and waiting.

You finally run out of ammunition. Your hands ache and you feel as though you're not part of your own body. When you look around, the others are dead. The soldier who called you a fool is beside you. Most of his head is gone. Numb, you search the bodies for usable supplies. As evening comes, the battle slows down.

Shiloh was the sixth bloodiest battle in American history.

45

Turn the page.

It starts to rain, so you cover yourself with a dead man's coat and try to sleep. The next day is the same. For hours you load and shoot. Your hands grow tired and your eyes burn. Sometimes you see a flash of the enemy's gray uniform through the smoke.

In the afternoon a cavalry officer appears. "The enemy is retreating!" he shouts as he gallops past. You drop your gun in relief. The Battle of Shiloh is over, and you survived.

THE END

To follow another path, turn to page 9.

To read the conclusion, turn to page 103.

If it were you, you would want someone to help you. You pick up a wounded soldier and put him on your back. He cries out in pain, although you try to be gentle. You stumble toward the river. By the time you get there, the man is dead. You set him down next to thousands of other dead and wounded soldiers sprawled along the riverbank. The ground seems to be an ocean of bleeding blue.

Soldiers continue to stagger out of the woods by the hundreds. The cries of downed men are all you hear. If you join the battle, this is what you'll become. It is best to stay here, hiding among the bodies, cowardly but alive.

THE END

To follow another path, turn to page 9.

To read the conclusion, turn to page 103.

48

Confederate troops with a huge Parrott gun

3
ROLLING OUT THE
BIG GUNS

When you enlisted in 1861, war fever was everywhere. Whole towns signed up to fight. You were swept away in waves of excitement.

At first it was the grand adventure everyone said it would be. You were assigned to artillery. You learned to shoot the big cannons, and you were good at it. So good that you were promoted to first sergeant—a great honor, not to mention better pay. First sergeants earn $20 a month!

Now it's 1863 and the "adventure" is long over. You've been in several battles and survived. But many of the men you enlisted with are dead. How much longer can your luck last?

Turn the page.

The army has been camped for some time. New recruits arrive every day. It's your job to train the new artillery soldiers before they get called to fight. Most of them don't want to be here. They were conscripted into service against their will. You don't care, though. You are determined to make them the best artillerymen in the army. A battle is brewing near Chattanooga—will they be ready in time?

To fight with Union artillery, go to page 51.

To be a Confederate artilleryman, turn to page 63.

"Attention!"

"Today is the first day of your life in an artillery battery," you begin. "A battery is a unit of either four or six cannons. It's our job to support the infantry and cause as much damage as we can to the enemy. Each gun is hooked up to a wagon called a limber," you continue. "The wagon holds an ammunition chest and water buckets. Six horses pull each limber."

You walk behind the limber and cannon. There is a four-wheeled cart here. "This here's the caisson. It carries two more ammunition chests. It's also got spare parts, wheels, and tools in case anything breaks down. The caisson attaches to the limber with this long pole."

51

To drill the recruits on the different kinds of cannons, turn to page 52.

To switch to artillery ammunition, turn to page 54.

"When are we going to shoot?" one recruit asks. His eyes are bright with excitement.

"Hold your horses," you say. "We'll shoot when I'm finished here." You point to the cannons sitting in a row. "You'll most likely fire either the Napoleon or the Parrott."

Your commanding officer comes over to watch you. "The 12-pound bronze Napoleons are fine weapons," he says, patting one fondly. He nods to you after giving the cannon a final pat. "Carry on."

Napoleon cannons had a range of more than 1,600 yards. Each could fire twice a minute.

Stepping to the next one, you continue. "This is a Parrott gun. It was named after the man who invented it, Robert Parker Parrott. It's a good gun, but you have to watch out. Sometimes they explode."

"Now, the Parrott might be dangerous, but it's also more accurate than the Napoleon," you explain. "Do you see these spiral grooves inside the gun's barrel? This is a new thing, called rifling. The grooves twist the ammunition as it shoots out, making it fly faster and more accurately. Napoleons are smoothbore, which means the inside of the barrel is smooth. Napoleons are not as accurate, but they're faster and easier to load."

"Now it's time to practice firing. Choose a cannon and step up."

To fire the Napoleon, turn to page 57.

To fire the Parrott, turn to page 59.

53

"We've got four kinds of ammunition shot," you begin. "They're solid, shell, case, and canister. Notice that they're all different shapes."

"Does it matter which shape we use?" one recruit asks.

"Good question," you say. "The shapes are specific to each cannon."

You point to two cast iron balls. "This here is solid shot. It comes in two shapes—round and elongated. The Napoleon fires the round shot. The elongated shot is for rifled cannons like the Parrott. Solid shot smashes through a battery, buildings, or large army formations."

You pause as the recruits examine the ammunition. "Solid shot fired from the Napoleon will bounce along the ground. If you see a metal ball coming your way, do not try to kick or stop it with your leg. It'll take your foot right off."

You kick the shot and scream, falling to the ground. The recruits gasp, but before anyone can move you jump up, perfectly fine. Everyone laughs nervously. You never get tired of that joke!

Still chuckling, you continue. "Next up are shells. They look like big bullets. They are hollow and are filled with black powder and a fuse. They explode into pieces above the enemy's head. They are good against enemy artillery."

Soldiers posed with explosive shells and heavy artillery called mortars.

Turn the page.

"Case shot looks similar to shells, but with thinner walls. It's filled with lead or iron balls and explosive chemicals. The flying balls and bits of metal from case shot are called shrapnel, after the British army officer who invented it."

You've saved the best for last. "Finally, there are canisters—the deadliest ammo we've got."

"They look like big tin cans," one recruit says.

"That's about right," you reply. "They are filled with iron balls and sawdust. When fired, the hot iron rains down on the enemy. You can load two canisters at once for even more damage."

56

The recruits spend the rest of their drill loading and firing. The captain appears and tells you that orders have come down. These men are moving out. It's sooner than you would like, but you don't get a say.

Turn to page 60.

The recruits practice loading and firing the beautiful bronze Napoleon. But they can't hit the target.

"Every time you miss, you give the enemy another chance to send cannon fire your way," you say, shaking your head.

The captain comes over to see what is wrong. He says he's taking over. "Go out into the field and take notes on where the shells are landing," he orders.

The break is a relief. There's a clump of trees alongside the field. That should be a safe place to watch. You climb the tallest tree and signal that you're ready. The recruits aim, fire, and BAM—the shell explodes above your head. Tree branches, leaves, and twigs crash down as you scramble out of the tree. Dizzy and bleeding, you make it back to camp.

Turn the page.

"Sir," you stammer, "May I ask permission to die by the enemy, instead of by friendly fire?" Then you collapse.

You wake up in the hospital tent. Half your face is bandaged, but you can see the captain and doctor through your good eye.

"The ammunition was bad," the captain says. "We never know it's bad until we fire it. Some of the shell grazed your face."

"Your eye is gone, and the right side of your face is paralyzed," the doctor says. "You're lucky it wasn't your whole head." You don't feel lucky.

58

"Thank you for your sacrifice," the captain says formally as he hands you some papers. "You're headed home."

THE END

To follow another path, turn to page 9.

To read the conclusion, turn to page 103.

The recruits practice loading and firing. You're proud of these new soldiers. They work hard and want to learn. Maybe they'll make good artillerymen after all.

"One more Confederate in the ground, and one more free slave!" one man hollers, as he tips in the ammunition. The other men's cheers are drowned out by the boom of the cannon.

"One more, boys, then we'll break," you say. They load the cannon, then you shout "FIRE!" Suddenly the barrel of the cannon explodes, sending hot metal everywhere. One piece slices through your uniform and into your chest. You're dead before they can get you to the camp surgeon.

59

THE END

To follow another path, turn to page 9.

To read the conclusion, turn to page 103.

The army marches for days until you arrive near Chattanooga, Tennessee. The land is rough and heavily forested, making it hard to get the cannons in place. The battery lines up on a ridge. You're sweating, but you don't know if it's from the heat or fear.

The battle starts without warning. A shell explodes nearby, throwing dirt everywhere. Soon the ground shakes from the roar of cannon fire. Shot and shell zoom overhead. Your men look terrified, but they load and shoot at the rebel army. It's not long before the cannon's ammunition in the nearby limber chest is gone.

You take several soldiers and dash to the caisson down the hill. The cart holds two more ammunition chests. A single chest weighs more than 500 pounds fully packed.

"C'mon boys!" you shout over the din of gunfire. "Every piece of ammo in this chest has a rebel's name on it!"

You and your men struggle to carry the chest as hot lead balls rain down around you. Once you get it back to the cannon you continue loading and firing. Trees and grass around the battery catch fire, but you hardly notice. "Stand your ground!" you shout.

In addition to enemy fire, soldiers risked injury from exploding cannons.

Turn the page.

You exchange cannon fire with the rebels for hours. The sun begins to fade and the battle slows down. Suddenly a loud explosion throws you off your feet. When you try to get up, you can't. Your men kneel on the ground in a circle. Some are crying. You don't feel any pain, but you're very tired.

"Took both legs clean off," you hear one of the soldiers whisper.

"Don't stop fighting!" you say. "Give those rebels the best you have left!" Then you close your eyes and leave this world.

THE END

To follow another path, turn to page 9.

To read the conclusion, turn to page 103.

Last year, in 1862, the Confederate government passed a conscription law. Every man between 18 and 35 was drafted into the army for three years. Later the draft ages changed to include men between 17 and 50. Some of the boys look barely old enough to hold a gun. Others have gray hair and stooped shoulders.

"Attention soldiers!" you shout. They all snap to attention. "You have been assigned to the artillery. You're going to shoot some Yankees!" Everyone bursts into cheers. When they're quiet, you continue.

63

You begin explaining the makeup of each battery and the requirements for each cannon. "We've also got a forge, a wagon of supplies, and six to eight caissons full of extra ammunition," you say as you make your way up and down the line of soldiers.

Turn the page.

a cannon and caisson being moved into position

You stop in front of a young, bored-looking man. "Are you sleeping?" you ask, peering into his face. "Am I boring you? The Yankees have cannons too. Wake up and learn to shoot back or they'll get you first!"

"Some of you will learn how to shoot the cannons," you continue. "The rest of you will take care of the horses and equipment."

To train the cannoneers, go to page 65.

To train the spare men, turn to page 68.

64

The eight men you've picked watch closely as the cannon crew shows them how to load and fire. Each person on the crew has a specific job. First two men unhook the gun from the limber and roll it into position. The gunner decides how far to shoot and which ammunition to use. He tells the runners, who fetch it.

The runners hand the ammo to a soldier standing beside the muzzle. He puts a bag of gunpowder and the ammunition inside the cannon. Another soldier has his thumb on the hole near the back of the cannon. This keeps the air out while the round is loaded. Any air could cause a premature spark, sending the ammunition—and the man loading it—flying.

Turn the page.

A soldier pushes the gunpowder and ammunition into the cannon with a ramrod. A thin, sharp metal wire is slid into the vent to puncture the black powder bag. Then a primer is placed in the vent. The primer makes a spark that explodes the gunpowder and fires the gun. When the gun goes off, the explosion sends it rolling backward.

The force of firing sent cannons recoiling backwards. They needed to be repositioned after every shot.

Another soldier watches to see how accurate the shot is. He tells the gunner, who can re-aim the cannon for the next shot.

You spend hours showing the new recruits how to load and fire. Finally they seem to understand what to do. And lucky for them—the orders come, and it's off to war. It's always the same story—recruits are pushed through training then shipped off to fight. But they don't always get enough time to learn their jobs. You'll just have to do your best to lead them through real battle when it comes.

67

Turn to page 69.

You pick the oldest and youngest men. "You might think these are the dull jobs," you tell them. "But each of you are important. If the horses are killed in battle, we can't move the cannons. If the cannoneers die, you will be spares to take their places."

"The guns look old and worn," a recruit says. "This one looks like it's from a Yankee factory."

"That's because it is," you reply. "We didn't have many cannons when the war started. When we win a battle, we win the cannons too. All of our guns in this battery are Union-made."

The men spend the day learning how to take care of the horses during battle and to repair the wagons and cannons. As you're finishing for the day, the captain approaches. "We're heading for Chattanooga, Tennessee," he says. "There's a big fight coming."

You meet up with the Army of Tennessee a few miles from Chattanooga. A man greets you. It's General Braxton Bragg. "The Union army drove him out of Chattanooga," someone whispers. "He's sworn to re-take the city."

A few days later, the battle begins. But you're ordered to remain behind as reinforcements.

That is not what your men wanted to hear. They wanted to kill Yankees! As the battle wears on, rumors fly through camp. First one side is winning. Then the other. Finally you get the orders to march. It's about time!

69

The battery rumbles through thick woods. "These Yankees have no business coming down here, telling us what to do," one soldier says.

"If we want to secede, it's our right to," another agrees.

Turn the page.

"Our way of life is our business!" a third man thunders. "Who are the Yankees to change it?"

Suddenly a huge blast shakes the trees. Cannon fire hits the battery. A horse goes down, blocking the road. No one can move. Your battery is an open target for the Yankee artillery.

You're all going to die unless someone moves that dead horse.

Artillery horses were exposed during battle. Crippling or killing the horses meant the enemy's guns couldn't advance.

To stay with the guns, go to page 71.

To move the horse, turn to page 72.

You order your men to leave the horse. But then another blast rocks the battery. Men and horses fly in all directions.

You see something out of the corner of your eye and instinctively raise your hand to block it. You turn to your men, but before you can say anything, one of them grabs you.

"You're hurt, sir," he says, horror in his voice. You look down at your arm. Your right hand is gone, and blood is pouring out of the stump. You must have tried to block a piece of shrapnel.

You hold your arm against your body so he can't see. "Get the men to safety," you say. Then you close your eyes. It is an honor to die in battle for the glory of the Confederacy.

THE END

To follow another path, turn to page 9.

To read the conclusion, turn to page 103.

The horse is heavy but you and three other soldiers are able to move it. You reach the edge of a field. The Yankees are directly ahead. It's time!

You exchange cannon fire with the Yankee battery. The air fills with smoke and the smell of gunpowder and blood. You hear a Yankee officer yell, "C'mon boys! Every piece of ammo in this chest has a rebel's name on it!" This makes your blood boil. You fire a round of case shot his way.

A shell hits one of the nearby guns with a fiery explosion. Horses and men are torn apart by the blast. An arm hits you in the head, spattering blood everywhere. The spare men run forward to take the places of the dead cannoneers. One boy struggles to load the cannon. He said he was 17 when he joined up, but he looks years younger.

72

To help the spare men, go to page 73.

To catch the runaway horses, turn to page 75.

"Let me help," you say, pushing the shell into the cannon.

The boy grins, despite a bloody wound on his shoulder. "I'm killing Yankees!" he crows as he runs to the caisson for more ammunition. What's left of the cannoneer team fights until the Yankee line is quiet.

The Battle of Chattanooga took place on November 23–25. The Union was victorious all three days, forcing the Confederates to withdraw.

Turn the page.

By now it's starting to get dark. Slowly you and the other survivors gather the few horses that are left. They'll pull the cannons back to camp. But there aren't enough horses to pull all of them. So you and the men pull the heavy cannons yourselves. It's slow going, and your legs ache with fatigue, but you make it back.

"What's that there?" a soldier points to your leg. To your complete shock, there is a jagged hole in your thigh. In the chaos of battle you never even noticed you were hurt.

"No wonder pulling the cannon was so hard," you think as you pass out.

74

Turn to page 76.

One horse is still hitched to the limber, which is filled with ammunition. The driver is dead. Another blast explodes so close that it knocks you down. The horse spooks and jumps forward. The limber jumps too. One of the wheels runs over your leg. Something cracks and you feel a rush of blinding pain. Everything goes dark.

Turn the page.

Somewhere near Chattanooga, Tennessee:

Dearest Sister,

We have been in a big fight, and my leg was hurt. Thanks be to God, I am still on this Earth. The first day of battle was hot work. Many of my soldiers were honorably killed doing their duty. Most of the horses were killed or ran away.

The second day was different. After a hard day of fighting on Lookout Mountain, we drove the Yankees back. It looked as though we had won, but we were ordered to withdraw to Missionary Ridge.

By the last day we thought we had a chance of holding back the Union. Many of us thought General Bragg would order us to finish the Yankees, but he didn't. We thought him a fool for not taking advantage, especially when they returned with reinforcements. We were soon overwhelmed and had to fall back.

We lost several good guns and many caissons and limbers before retreating.

My injury kept me from helping to bury the dead. The others dug a pit and rolled each dead man in his blanket and buried them all together. All of the dead were killed by artillery fire. Almost no one died from rifle shots.

I think we will stay here for a while. I have been given a leave for 30 days because of my injury. Look for me on the Wednesday train.

Your loving brother …

THE END

To follow another path, turn to page 9.

To read the conclusion, turn to page 103.

The idea of a heroic Confederate cavalry rider ready to lead a raid or rush to the frontline was a popular one in the South.

4
DEADLY RIDERS

At the start of the war, not everyone thought cavalry soldiers would be necessary. They were expensive, and some generals didn't know what to do with them. Union leaders believed it took two years to train a good cavalry, and they expected the war to be over before then.

But the Confederate army understood the cavalry's value. Cavalry riders make great scouts and can travel much farther and faster than men on foot. Middle- and upper-class Confederate men learned to ride at a young age, and many already owned at least one horse.

Turn the page.

The rebel cavalry forces were deadly during the first years of the war. The Union figured out that they needed a strong cavalry too. Eventually both sides developed strong cavalry units.

For three years you have been receiving letters from your brothers who are fighting in the war. They tell awe-inspiring stories of battles and adventures. You have just turned 17. It's finally your chance to join in!

Both of your brothers fight from horseback. You also want to be a cavalry soldier. The idea of riding into battle is thrilling.

80

To ride with the Confederate cavalry, go to page 81.

To join a Union cavalry unit, turn to page 93.

A poster in the general store says there is a recruiting meeting today in the church. When you get there, only a few people fill the pews. Most of them are young boys like you, or older men.

A tired-looking officer in a worn gray uniform sits in front. "General Lee has need of cavalry reinforcements," he says. He tells you that your pay will be $12 a month, plus an extra forty cents a day for the use of your horse.

You'll have to provide your own horse. "If your horse is killed in battle, the government will pay you for it, but you are responsible for replacing it," he explains. "We often capture horses, but you can't count on those. If yours is captured, worn out, or disabled, you have to pay for another one or be moved to another part of the army."

81

Turn the page.

"What about weapons and uniforms?" you ask. The officer frowns.

"You'll bring your own weapons until the army can provide you with more," he says. "Mostly we take weapons and supplies off dead Yankees."

You sign a paper. "Welcome to the war," he says solemnly. "There isn't time for training. The Army of Northern Virginia, led by Robert E. Lee, needs reinforcements in Jeb Stuart's cavalry. I also hear Nathan Bedford Forrest is looking for a few good men to ride with his outfit."

To join the Army of Northern Virginia, go to page 83.
To join Nathan Bedford Forrest's raiders, turn to page 85.

Several new recruits and a few veterans travel together. You're so excited. The Army of Northern Virginia! You'll be fighting in the biggest, strongest Confederate army, under Robert E. Lee himself.

"Don't get too excited. You'll be lucky to see any action," one veteran says. "Mostly, cavalry regiments are used for security. We do guard duty, protect civilians, and scout. Sometimes we go on raids. We also protect the army during retreats."

The Army of Northern Virginia just won a big battle in Chancellorsville. The troops are in high spirits. Your group is directed to the officer's area. A young man with long beard meets you.

"That's Jeb Stuart himself," someone whispers. "He stopped John Brown's army at Harpers Ferry and has fought Indians too."

Turn the page.

James Elwell Brown ("J. E. B." or "Jeb") Stuart resigned his U.S. army post in 1861 to join the Confederacy.

"I hope you're ready for some fighting. I have orders from General Lee," Stuart says, looking hard at his new troops. "He's marching the army into Union territory. Some cavalry will scout the area for Yankees. I also need a security detail to escort wounded soldiers to the hospital train."

To go on the scouting mission, turn to page 86.

To escort the wounded, turn to page 87.

Nathan Bedford Forrest is the most famous cavalry commander in the Confederacy. You've heard all the stories. Before the war he was a wealthy businessman. When the fighting began, he used his own money to raise a unit. For the last three years he's become the most feared horseback commander in the Confederate army. It's no wonder they call him the "wizard of the saddle."

When you finally meet him, he peers at you with sharp eyes. "It seems the Yankees have been ordered to destroy Confederate factories and supplies in Rome, Georgia. We can't let that happen. I need some scouts to ride ahead and tell me how many Yankee troops are coming. I also need a small cavalry force to fall back and watch the rear of the Yankee army. Who will volunteer?"

To ride ahead and scout, turn to page 90.

To fall back, turn to page 92.

The scouting mission starts before dawn. You and the other riders explore the area west of the army. General Stuart doesn't want General Lee to run into any surprise Union troops.

Hours later the sun blazes overhead. No one has seen any Yankees. As the tired group heads back to camp, your horse stumbles, sending you to the ground. You're dizzy and disoriented when you come to. "My … horse … " you mumble.

"It broke its shoulder when it fell," a foggy shape says. "I'm sorry. We couldn't save it."

The world is spinning and there's blood in your eyes. You're boosted onto a spare horse and led back to camp. You're injured and your horse is dead. Your cavalry career is over.

THE END

To follow another path, turn to page 9.

To read the conclusion, turn to page 103.

The wounded men are being loaded onto wagons when you arrive. Many are carried on rough stretchers. You can't stand the sight of people without arms or legs. When you look at them, all you can think of is bloody amputation saws and the pain the men must have felt as the army surgeon worked on them.

You wonder what will become of these soldiers once they get home. Some of them can't walk, let alone plow a field or do any kind of labor. And if the Confederacy loses the war, there won't even be slaves to do the heavy work.

It's a few miles to the hospital train, and the wagons move slowly. The stench of death and infection makes your stomach heave. A few men have bayonet or saber wounds. More have injuries from cannons. But most of the wounds were caused by minié balls.

Turn the page.

Hospital trains were special cars used to transport wounded soldiers to medical care facilities.

No part of the body is safe from injury. One man had a bullet hit him in the head. It entered through his left cheek and came out on the right side of his chin. His face looks like raw meat.

You see men with arm and leg damage, head wounds, and chest and abdominal injuries. Some of the wounds smell rotten. You think dying in battle would be better than surviving this way.

After the last afflicted man is loaded onto the train, you dismount and gently stroke your horse's smooth coat. A small boy rushes past and you grab his shoulder. When he turns, you press a coin in his hand.

"Make sure this horse gets back to the army," you whisper. The boy nods and leads the horse away. When he's gone, you slip into the train car and find a spot among the wounded. For deserting, you might be whipped, your head shaved, and your pay taken away. And, although unlikely, you might even face a death sentence. But you are willing to take the chance if that means keeping your limbs and staying alive—for as long as possible.

89

THE END

To follow another path, turn to page 9.

To read the conclusion, turn to page 103.

For three days you spy on Union soldiers. Local people helpfully tell you everything they know about the hated Yankees. The army is almost 2,000 strong, but their commander, Colonel Streight, has given his infantry men mules to ride. You laugh just thinking about it.

Mules are often used to pull artillery and supply wagons. But they are temperamental and not ideal cavalry mounts. You think the Union soldiers look ridiculous riding them to war, and you refer to them as the "Jackass Cavalry."

Over dinner, the loud bray of a mule tied nearby startles you. It gives you an idea. You ride into Nashville, where the mules are being held. Quietly you open the corrals, and then start shouting. The mules stampede!

You all laugh as the sorry-looking animals bolt out of the enclosures and scatter. It will take Streight's men days to round them all up.

Forrest roars when he hears what you have done. "That's what I like to see," he says. "I think you'll do fine in my unit."

THE END

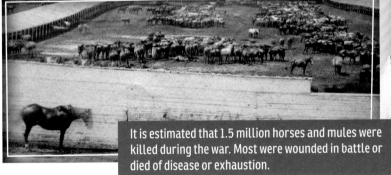

It is estimated that 1.5 million horses and mules were killed during the war. Most were wounded in battle or died of disease or exhaustion.

To follow another path, turn to page 9.

To read the conclusion, turn to page 103.

The Yankees are riding mules instead of horses. You and the others start calling them the "Mule Brigade." For days you follow the army, attacking when you can. The Union army is far bigger than Forrest's small force, but that doesn't seem to matter to your commander. He orders you to chase Streight's army all the way to the edge of Rome, Georgia.

When the Union army stops for rest, you swarm in. They are so exhausted from riding the mules that they don't fight back. Some even fall asleep while you shoot at them! Forrest demands surrender, and Streight agrees. You've won your first big cavalry battle.

THE END

To follow another path, turn to page 9.

To read the conclusion, turn to page 103.

It's funny how a few months can change things. Riding into battle sounded heroic when the war started. Then long casualty lists began appearing in the newspaper. Then the draft letter comes with news—it's your turn to go to war.

There might be a way to get out of fighting. Your father has enough money to hire a substitute to fight in your place. Or you could lie and say that you are mentally disabled or that you are the only son of a widow. But Father won't let you do it. "I'm not paying $300 so someone else can steal your glory," he says. "It's your duty to fight. Just like your brothers."

When you reluctantly report for duty, the officer looks at you. "Can you ride?" he asks. "Many new cavalry recruits have never been on a horse."

To say yes, turn to page 94.

To say no, turn to page 95.

It's not exactly a lie. You've hopped rides on carriage or plow horses here and there.

You might have been able to fool the officer, but you can't fool the horse. As soon as it feels your foot in the stirrup, it dances sideways. Then the saddle slips. The horse bolts. You hang on for a moment, but the horse passes too close to a tree and scrapes you off. The moment your arm hits the tree, you know something is wrong.

You limp back to the unimpressed officer, who can see that your arm is broken.

94

Your family just got word that your brothers are missing in action. That's enough to convince Father to spend the $300 on a substitute. You'll finish out the war at home, praying for your brothers' return.

THE END

To follow another path, turn to page 9.

To read the conclusion, turn to page 103.

"Glad you admitted it. Some of these horses have never been handled. A green rider could be killed," the officer says.

The officer assigns you a sturdy, gentle horse. The commander gives everyone shiny new sabers. It's tricky to use it without cutting yourself, stabbing the man next to you, or slicing off your horse's ears. But you're a fast learner, and your horse keeps its ears.

On inspection day, you demonstrate using your saber and firing a revolver from horseback. Now you're a real cavalryman. Your blue uniform looks splendid. Its brass buttons gleam in the sun. Your orders are to join General Buford's cavalry division as part of the biggest Union force, known as the Army of the Potomac. They have been in several big battles and they need reinforcements.

Turn the page.

The Pennsylvania countryside is beautiful, but you don't have time to admire it. You hear about the Battle of Brandy Station, a huge cavalry battle that was fought nearby. The Union army has been gathering their forces here since then. As soon as your new group of cavalry recruits arrive, General Buford appears. Soon you, along with 3,000 other cavalrymen, are lined up and ready to listen.

"Men!" Buford barks. "We are headed to a little town nearby called Gettysburg. I'm looking for the rebel army. I need a few scouts to ride ahead. The rest will come with me."

To scout ahead, go to page 97.
To stay with General Buford, turn to page 98.

The sleepy town of Gettysburg looks peaceful. There's no sign of the Confederate forces. But a dust cloud in the distance catches your eye. You can just make out a handful of patrol riders galloping away. They're too far away to shoot at and too far ahead to pursue.

General Buford thinks a big fight is coming. He orders Colonel Tom Devin to set up several groups of scouts, called pickets, around the town.

"I don't think there will be many rebels coming," Devin says skeptically.

The general shakes his head. "They will attack from the north and the west," he says. You believe him. "We are outnumbered, but we can stand firm. You will have to fight like the devil until support arrives."

To stay with General Buford, turn to page 98.

To join the picket, turn to page 100.

No one gets any sleep. Early the next morning, the unit lines up in rows. The impact of the Confederate army rushing together on foot shakes the ground like an explosion.

With a shout your unit dismounts and shoots at the Confederates. The air fills with gunfire. Artillery fire rains down, but you manage to avoid getting killed. Soldiers and horses fall all around you, but you keep shooting. Your own horse has disappeared.

General Buford's strategy slowed the Confederates' advance and allowed the rest of the Union army enough time to arrive at Gettysburg.

The Confederates keep fighting, but they can't advance. By the end of the day it's clear that they aren't going to. The cavalry did what it was ordered to do: keep the Confederates busy until the rest of the army could arrive. Everyone cheers as your unit returns to camp.

"Well done," General Buford says, smiling. "You have faced a heavy task today, and you performed admirably. I am sending all of you to guard supply lines tomorrow. You've earned a rest for your bravery in battle."

There's no arguing with the general, so you head out. A rest will feel good, but you know that you'll soon be back.

THE END

To follow another path, turn to page 9.
To read the conclusion, turn to page 103.

The Battle of Gettysburg was the largest and bloodiest battle in U.S. history, with around 51,000 casualties.

To the family of this brave cavalryman,

It is with deepest sadness that I must tell you that your son has given his life for the cause of liberty and freedom. He was under my command during the great battle at Gettysburg, and I would like to tell you what a brave and honorable man he showed himself to be.

He held the Union line throughout the night before the battle. In the morning, the Confederates attacked. Although we were badly outnumbered, your son did not flinch. In the smoke and heat of battle he met the enemy. He killed many rebels before he was struck by a rebel ball. I am sending his effects in the enclosed box. I was proud to serve with him, as you should be proud of his sacrifice.

General John Buford

THE END

To follow another path, turn to page 9.

To read the conclusion, turn to page 103.

Around 620,000 soldiers died during the Civil War. Two-thirds died from disease. Eighty percent of the remaining men were killed by rifles.

5
NOTHING IS THE SAME

The Civil War changed the way war was fought. People on both sides of the battle line were shocked at the unimaginable death and injury. Before the war, guns could not shoot far. Bullet wounds were less fatal. War was still terrible, but not as bloody. The Civil War changed all of that.

A few years before the war, the way guns were made changed forever. Spiral grooves inside the gun barrel made the bullets spin as they were shot. The grooves, called rifling, shot bullets farther and more accurately. When paired with another pre-war invention, the minié ball, rifling became deadly.

Minié balls could be loaded quickly and fired true. They tore into the body, doing terrible damage. Minié balls would also flatten on contact, damaging flesh and breaking bone.

Before the war, armies would line up and face each other on the field of battle. They had to get close enough for their weapons to hit each other. Rifling and the minié ball made that tactic deadly.

Big guns like the Napoleon and the Parrott were dangerous too, with their ammunition canisters and shrapnel shells. Commanders on both sides were slow to realize that their military training was outdated and ineffective against these new inventions. Only after war was over did they understand this mistake.

Although the Union won the war, commanders on both sides became famous for their bravery, intelligence, and leadership.

Confederate Nathan Bedford Forrest was never captured or defeated by any Union force. He was wounded four times and had 29 horses shot out from under him. Robert E. Lee, the commander of the Army of Northern Virginia, became the president of Washington and Lee University after the war.

Union commander Ulysses S. Grant was the only general who figured out how to defeat Robert E. Lee and win the war. He was elected president of the United States in 1868. John Buford, a Union hero at Gettysburg, died of typhoid fever in December 1863, only a few months after his victory at Gettysburg.

Around 620,000 men lost their lives fighting for the North and South. A century and a half later, America's bloodiest conflict is still the Civil War.

TIMELINE

November 6, 1860—Abraham Lincoln is elected president of the United States.

December 20, 1860—South Carolina becomes the first state to secede from the Union.

April 12–13, 1861—Confederate troops attack Union-held Fort Sumter, starting the Civil War.

July 21, 1861—The First Battle of Manassas (also called the Battle of Bull Run) is fought in Virginia. Colonel Thomas Jackson earns the nickname "Stonewall" for his bravery during battle.

November 6, 1861—Jefferson Davis is elected the president of the Confederate States of America.

March 9, 1862—The first battle between ironclad warships is fought between the USS *Monitor* and CSS *Virginia*.

April 6–7, 1862—Union victory at the Battle of Shiloh. More than 23,000 men are killed in action.

August 29–30, 1862—The Second Battle of Manassas is fought, resulting in a Confederate victory.

September 16–18, 1862—The Army of the Potomac attacks Robert E. Lee's forces in Maryland at the Battle of Antietam. The Union victory forces the Confederates out of Maryland.

January 1, 1863—President Lincoln delivers the Emancipation Proclamation. Slaves in Confederate states are now free.

March 3, 1863—Congress passes the conscription act. All men between the ages of 20 and 45 must register for the military.

April 26–May 3, 1863—Nathan Bedford Forrest's cavalry captures Colonel Abel Streight's mule train near Rome, Georgia.

July 1–3, 1863—The Battle of Gettysburg is fought. The Union wins, but at great cost. More than 50,000 soldiers from both armies are killed, wounded, or captured during the battle.

November 19, 1863—President Lincoln delivers the Gettysburg Address.

November 23–25, 1863—Union victory at Chattanooga.

May 11, 1864—Jeb Stuart is killed at the Battle of Yellow Tavern.

January 31, 1865—Congress abolishes slavery.

April 9, 1865—Robert E. Lee surrenders the Army of Northern Virginia, ending the war.

April 14, 1865—President Lincoln is assassinated.

OTHER PATHS TO EXPLORE

In this book you've seen three different battles from three points of view. Perspectives on history are as varied as the people who lived it. Seeing history from many points of view is an important part of understanding it.

Here are some ideas for other Civil War points of view to explore:

1. Many older soldiers had fought in the Mexican-American War (1846–1848). With all the new inventions introduced during the Civil War—such as ironclad ships, submarines, hot air balloons, the telegraph, and railroads—how would their war experiences have changed? (Integration of Knowledge and Ideas)

2. During the war, Dr. Richard Gatling invented the first machine gun. The Gatling gun could fire 400 rounds a minute. But no one wanted to use it, and it did not become popular until the war was over. How would you feel knowing this weapon could change the war—but being unable to use it? (Integration of Knowledge and Ideas)

3. Maryland, Kentucky, Delaware, and Missouri were slave states that chose not to join the Confederacy. What would life have been like for slaves and slaveholders living in these states? (Key Ideas and Details)

READ MORE

Allen, Thomas B. *Mr. Lincoln's High-Tech War.* Washington, D.C.: National Geographic Children's Books, 2009.

Fein, Eric. *Weapons, Gear, and Uniforms of the Civil War.* Equipped for Battle. North Mankato, Minn.: Capstone Press, 2012.

Stanchak, John. *Eyewitness Civil War.* Eyewitness Books. New York: DK Eyewitness Books, 2011.

INTERNET SITES

Use FactHound to find Internet sites related to this book. All of the sites on FactHound have been researched by our staff.

Here's all you do:
Visit *www.facthound.com*
Type in this code: 9781491421499

GLOSSARY

abolish (uh-BOL-ish)—to put an end to something officially

artillery (ar-TI-luhr-ee)—large guns, such as cannons or missile launchers, that require several soldiers to load, aim, and fire

battery (BAT-uh-ree)—a group of heavy guns that are all used together

cartridge (KAHR-trij)—a container that holds the gunpowder, primer, and ammunition for a gun

casualty (KAZH-oo-uhl-tee)—someone who is injured, captured, killed, or missing in an accident, a disaster, or a war

conscript (kuhn-SKRIPT)—a forced military draft

draft (DRAFT)—to select someone to serve in the military

enlist (en-LIST)—to voluntarily join a branch of the military

foundry (FOUN-dree)—a factory for melting and shaping metal

fuse (FYOOZ)—a cord or wick that can burn from end to end

infantry (IN-fuhn-tree)—a group of soldiers trained to fight and travel on foot

pacifist (PASS-uh-fist)—a person who believes that war is wrong

quartermaster (KWOR-tur-MASS-tur)—a military department of officer in charge of getting supplies to troops

recruit (ri-KROOT)—someone who joins a company or organization

rifling (RYE-fling)—grooves in the barrel of a gun that make the bullet travel farther and straighter

secede (si-SEED)—to formally withdraw from a group or organization, often to form another organization

shrapnel (SHRAP-nuhl)—pieces that have broken off from an explosive shell

skirmish (SKUR-mish)—a minor fight in a battle

tactic (TAK-tik)—a plan for fighting a battle

BIBLIOGRAPHY

Brown, Thaddeus C.S., Samuel J. Murphy, and William G. Putney. *Behind the Guns: The History of Battery I, 2nd Regiment, Illinois Light Artillery.* Carbondale: Southern Illinois University Press, 2000.

Burns, Vincent L. *The Fifth New York Cavalry in the Civil War.* Jefferson, N.C.: McFarland & Company, Inc., Publishers, 2014.

Davis, William C. *Fighting Men of the Civil War.* Norman: University of Oklahoma Press, 1998.

Heidler, David S., and Jeanne T. Heidler, eds. *Encyclopedia of the American Civil War: A Political, Social, and Military History.* Santa Barbara, Calif.: ABC-CLIO, 2000.

Hubbell, John T., and James W. Geary, eds. *Biographical Dictionary of the Union: Northern Leaders of the Civil War.* Westport, Conn.: Greenwood Press, 1995.

Hughes, Nathaniel Cheairs. *The Pride of the Confederate Artillery: The Washington Artillery in the Army of Tennessee.* Baton Rouge: Louisiana State University Press, 1997.

McKenney, Janice E. *The Organizational History of Field Artillery 1775–2003.* Washington, D.C.: Center of Military History, United States Army, 2007.

Thiele, Thomas Frederick. *The Evolution of Cavalry in the American Civil War, 1861–1863.* Ann Arbor, Mich.: University of Michigan, 1951.

Throne, Mildred, ed. *The Civil War Diary of Cyrus F. Boyd, Fifteenth Iowa Infantry, 1861–1863.* Baton Rouge: Louisiana State University Press, 1998.

Wiley, Bell Irvin. *The Life of Johnny Reb: The Common Soldier of the Confederacy.* Baton Rouge: Louisiana State University Press, 2008.

INDEX